Spot the Horseguard!

gumball 3000

THIS BOOK BELONGS TO

Name: _____

Car: _____

Title: Gumball 3000
Sub Title: The Official Annual 2006
www.gumball3000.com

ISBN 0-9547226-2-0
EAN 9 780954 722623

Published by:
Gumball 3000 Merchandise Limited
4 Lucerne Mews, London
W8 4ED, Great Britain

First Published: April 2006

Founders: Maximillion Cooper & Julie Brangstrup
Editor-In-Chief: Maximillion Cooper
Produced and Edited by: Duncan Scholes

Art Director: Tim Hutton
Main Writer: Maximillion Cooper
Contributing Writers: Duncan Scholes & Nick Wyllys
Photo Editors: Tim Hutton, Nick Wyllys
Main Photographers: Jonathan Bushell, Dan Anslow, Fiona McLeod
Cuban Brothers/550LM Illustration: Nick Wavish
Gumball Puzzles: RHS
Captain Gumball Story: Barnaby Girling
Captain Gumball Illustration: SPZERO76
Gumball Dating Agency: Antony Adel
Proof Reading: Lucinda Cooper
Printed in the UK by Butler and Tanner

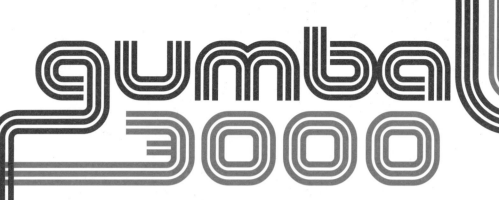

THE OFFICIAL ANNUAL 2006

CONTENTS

Jonathan Bushell

Maximillion's Ferrari General Lee tackles London Crowds

"Welcome fans...

...to the latest news, reviews, features and celebrity insights from the cockpit of the seventh annual 'Gumball 3000' Rally.

Back in January 1999, Gumball was my baby, and following the success of the first rally in the spring of that year it has continued to spawn into one of the most recognized and notorious events on sporting and celebrity calendars. By embracing cultures, and with an appeal beyond that of any 'normal' car rally, 'Gumball 3000' has combined the attributes of the action sports, fashion, music and film industries to create a unique lifestyle brand for everyone.

This annual will give you the inside stories from the road, and take you on the 3000 mile journey that took place in the spring of 2005, starting in London and finishing 7 days later in Monaco's Casino Square. Always asked the question, what's the best car on the rally? I thought I'd do my best 'Martin Brundle' impression and walk you down the pit-lane and give you my insight into the entry grid this year. The grid on the Gumball is always unique, and this year was no different, infact each year I'm amazed at the diversity of both car and driver; some opting for comfort, some for style, and others are just simply asking for trouble. I'm forever encouraged by the strugglers on the rally, those cars that sit uncomfortably on the starting grid even before the event has begun, suffering a constant onslaught of jokes at its capability of completing the Gumball! In 2004 the Citroen 2CV took this mantle. No one thought it would make it 3000 miles around Europe, let alone in 6 days or keep up with the supercars taking part. But with a lot of perseverance, and even more 'Gumball spirit', that humble vehicle (bought on ebay for $200) not only made its way round on time, but quite often it finished each stage mid-pack, having the last laugh each night at all those 'prancing horses' that appeared to have 'bolted off' too quickly!

Having set the example in '04 for all things slow and unreliable, in 2005 the back-packers were led from the rear by the incredulous 'Ice-Cream' van, complete with 'Green sleeves' playing as it arrived several hours late to each check-point, serving melted ice cream to passers by, completing the 3000 miles despite its top speed of just 50mph, and a mere 15mph up hills. Slightly ahead was the incredibly long 'Stretch Hummer', providing the 'non-stop' partying environment for The Cuban Brothers and soul diva Kym Mazelle; I can only imagine what went on in that car!

Just infront was a pack of roaring V8 American muscle cars, including a 1970 Buick Riviera, 1970 Dodge Challenger 440 R/T (complete with the world's largest in-car sound system!), and a Pontiac GT0, but sadly only two of these crossed the finish line on their own wheels, the others made it, but on the back of a 'trailer'. Ahead of these yanks were the most stylish group of 60s, 70s and 80s sports cars, including a stunning Aston Martin DB4, a V12 E-Type Jaguar, a 1990 Lamborghini Countach, and most beautiful of all, a 1963 Lola T70 MkIII. After this sat the lone Caterham 7. Everyone knows its fast, light and nimble on the road, but at only a couple of inches off the ground, and no roof, you can hear people thinking "I wouldn't want to do it in that!" Next up was the sheer 'luxury' department, headed by the Rolls Royce Phantom, and sprinkled with Bentley's, Brabus and AMG Mercedes, and towing the line close behind was an incredibly rare 1976 Bristol 411.

Now we've reached the 'top end', where a parade of supercars turn heads in awe; Ferrari, Lamborghini, McLaren, Koenigsegg, Farboud, Pagani, MB, 1963 VW Samba Split-Screen Camper van??!! (With nitros!), Porsche, and so on; more supercars than took part in Le Mans this year!
And as for my car, well, she was a real beauty. A 2003 Ferrari 550 Le Mans, tuned and prepared by Prodrive, and painted like the 'General Lee', in homage to the red neck friend of mine from Tennessee, Johnny Knoxville, starring in the Dukes of Hazzard movie. She drove like a dream...

Gumball 3000 Creator

Spot the difference

Nice Cars - No Crowds!!

What a difference 6 years makes...

Nice Cars - Nice Crowds!!

GUMBALL3000

Gumball 3000 Rally 2005 Route Map

London to Folkestone, Euro Tunnel
Calais to Belgium, Chateau d' acoz
Chateau d' acoz to Prague
Prague to Vienna
Vienna to Hungarian F1 circuit
F1 circuit to Budapest, roman baths
Budapest to Krka National Park, Sibenik
Sibenik to Dubrovnik.
Dubrovmik to Bari
Bari to Sicily
Sicily to Rome
Rome to Florence
Florence to Monaco

..., 6 days. 3000 miles.

2005

THE GRID

ENTER THE COMPETITION:

How much of a Gumball fan are you?! Email us at info@gumball3000.com with the names of all the cars that didn't make it to the finish line to win a big bag of Gumball goodies that will make your friends green with envy!!

Premiere Party

The night before the 2005 rally kicked off in Central London, we premiered the docufilm of the 2004 rally called '6 Days in May' to a VIP crowd of 3000 people. After the film, the night was packed full of your regular Gumball party entertainment...The Cuban Brothers, followed by soul legend Kym Mazelle, and then Tyler James, followed by Jamiroquai. The crowd went crazy when Jay Kay came on...he's a huge Gumball fan and was spotted at the end of the night drooling over the supercar display outside!

The Cat in the Hat entertains the crowd!

Cars & Stars all the way at the Gumball premiere party

GUMBALL 3000 '6 DAYS IN MAY'

DIRECTED BY RUBEN FLEISCHER

Why not throw your own premiere party, 6 Days in May is available now on DVD

The Cubans work their best catalogue pose

Peaches Geldof looking peachy

Love Actually star Martine McCutcheon and Sonia Cadman save you a front row seat!

Kill Bill star Daryl Hannah arrives straight from NY!

The Cuban Brothers

The Cuban Brothers are unique. Born of the loins of seventies Havana, nurtured on a diet of soulful, sexy tunes and inspired by Cuban historical fact and mythology, their fresh approach to live entertainment whips up a frenzy at every gig. Their legendary performance at the Gumball parties combines music, riotous comedy, both physical and observational, and sensational dancing - consequently the energy at every show is incredible! Having performed first on the Gumball in 2000, and subsequently driving and performing in the 2003 rally from San Francisco to Miami, and starring in

'Gumball 3000' - The Movie, they have become Gumball favourites. In 2005 they experienced the Gumball from the luxury of the Stretch Hummer, sleeping by day, and performing each night, with Miguel whipping the audience up into a screaming frenzy!

England
London

The Farboud GT LeMans car get
underway infront of thousands of onlooker

Under starters orders

Formnula 1 Ace Jenson Button waves the flag

And they're off.....

GO GO GO !!!!

Ferrari F40

Ben Rousseau

TECH SPEC

0-60 (mph): 3.7 secs

Max speed (mph): 201 mph

Max power: 478bhp

Miles per gallon: 15

Engine size: 2936cc

Cost new: $415,000

Total produced: 1315

Modifications: Not needed!!

The F40 is all performance with zero frills, it even has strings for door-pulls to save weight! This Supercar offered the buyer the closest thing to a Formula One driving experience as one could get in 1987!

This rare breed was driven on the rally by Neil Cooke:

"Everything went wrong in Croatia when we were maxed out charging after the Enzo, up to then it had been running sweet as a nut, but our luck ran out when she instantly lost half her power and flames came shooting out of the exhaust followed shortly after by a trail of thick black smoke. We pulled over pronto, grabbed our passports and jumped out of the smoking car- expecting the worst.

Fortunately, she didnt explode!!

The irony is that we had a joke on the rally that if she were to blow up, we would want her to blow up in the tunnel at Monaco, but unfortunately it didnt make it that far!

We arranged for her to be transported to the hotel in Rome where she was shipped back to the UK.

Back in the garage in the UK we stripped the car and rebuilt half the engine, adding bigger turbo's, a racing clutch and a straight through exhaust.

Hopefully the improved spec will make her the ultimate Gumball car for the 2006 Rally!!"

The F40 is a crowd magnet

All systems checked and ready to go

Mark ..., legendary dancer from the Happy Mondays first took part in the Gumball in 2000 in a Jaguar. This year he was back for more in the Scooby Doo van!!

Take a trip with Happy Mondays Star

BEZ

LIVE FAS
DIE HARI

Dan Anslow

Q&A with Bez

Car driven in Gumball?
Richie from Fuel's Dodge van - massive mistake - never going in it again!
Terrible top speed! 80mph and it kept boiling over too!

What would be your dream Gumball car?
I know what that would be...and am gonna bring it next year! Me very own pimped out taxi!!!

Any special modifications, if so how much?
The latest home movie entertainment system and an 'orgasmatic' seat in the back with 8 built in subs and stimulation equipment!!

Fiona McLeod enjoys the ...tron chair!

EXIDE MAXXIMA

SHOCKWAVE
THE LOUDEST BASS ON EARTH
888.com

H 615
DFG

Jonathan Bushell

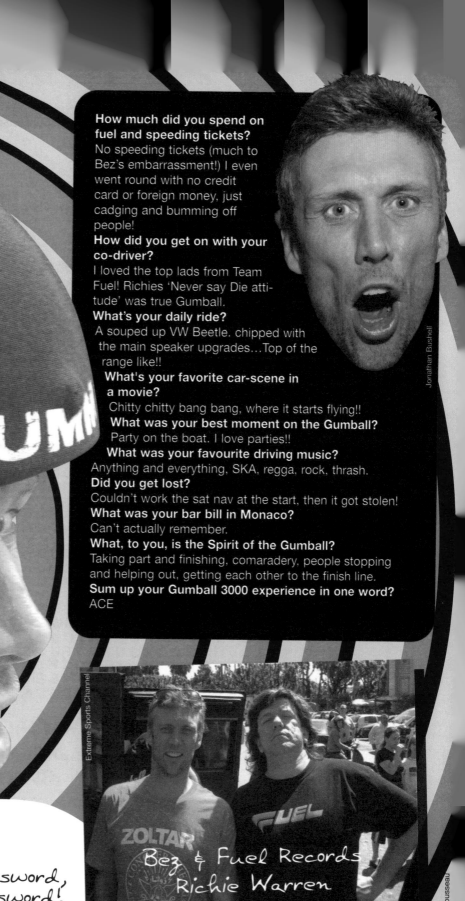

How much did you spend on fuel and speeding tickets?
No speeding tickets (much to Bez's embarrassment!) I even went round with no credit card or foreign money, just cadging and bumming off people!

How did you get on with your co-driver?
I loved the top lads from Team Fuel! Richies 'Never say Die attitude' was true Gumball.

What's your daily ride?
A souped up VW Beetle. chipped with the main speaker upgrades...Top of the range like!!

What's your favorite car-scene in a movie?
Chitty chitty bang bang, where it starts flying!!

What was your best moment on the Gumball?
Party on the boat. I love parties!!

What was your favourite driving music?
Anything and everything, SKA, regga, rock, thrash.

Did you get lost?
Couldn't work the sat nav at the start, then it got stolen!

What was your bar bill in Monaco?
Can't actually remember.

What, to you, is the Spirit of the Gumball?
Taking part and finishing, comaradery. people stopping and helping out, getting each other to the finish line.

Sum up your Gumball 3000 experience in one word?
ACE

Jonathan Bushell

Extreme Sports Channel

Bez & Fuel Records Richie Warren

Live by the sword, die by the sword!

Ben Rousseau

GUMBALL 3000 WORD SEARCH

```
Z W H G D Z O N N A J H S D F O E P Z D G H T L A T I
N A R Q I M A C D M C O N D A S X E A S E N Z O I K J
S L I R H S Y W U K S N Z E B Y Y T K B Z P D E F G R
E M I R P Q C P A I B Y I B T U D S V P A U H A I O U D
G R A C L D P P H O A O G M E T B Z N F A E I I W G Q
T C A R R E R A G T N N T L A L O A O S E A N C N M E
R P Q T I D S Y I L L U B T R X T O R N Z F T E D L M
S I G D G R T F A U Z T D R M A I T E R P I E C E P E
E A G M Q S R L L Y B S R I O H B M E T B R W R T O N
S L I H T Z A F G I T Y R O Y T V R I Z A E P E H E O
T S I H A W I T R O L L O L A T H I S L Z A O A K N D
C P O C R A L L Y R A I D U K H U E A U L D E M K S E
O T E A R T H U F O B B Z M E M Y S R L F I N V I Y R
K O D B G E T U I Z T E E H E E C R M S I T O A P S C
T S I U F R O D I S H A L L E I D U G O B I T N E A M
K R D K Z L U H F O X Z E C W O U E U D R S U J C I D
T D U B R O V N I K A M I T Y I R P M Q J V C Z D C I
G N I P Y O T E X J S R H Z R K T O B Y U I T O U M K
Q P R S T P A J Z X P F Z X Y L O H A U Q U Z D Y U I
N D U F F L G E N A D A U Q D U B R L S E N Z V V D S
Z N I S A A O F C U Z D G E N E R A L L E E S P O D H
Z E A G O C M U S N L P C D T A P A O U T N D Z N U I
U Z D E G E N E R I M N M Y T Z K O L M U A S D Z O M
G D O C E F T P I C B E D E R E M B A L L M P O F E O
K I S H I M O G E L L E R T B A T H S U Y D J A Z R T
U O F I P A N D A C E E N K R O Y E S P R L F G U T O
Q P B Z E E C I S P E C T I R M Q N B O E Z T O F B O
J D A V E C O U R T N E Y O K T W L O U U C D T Z A E
N D E C I U U H A S D O X O U X U X F U L L T O Z T S
U P I Z N E R I B H U X X O X G M O I P D K D R Z H E
X M O D A R Y L H A N N A H N T I P N E E F N C E F F
T G F C D G E H J Q G L N Z M B F O C O U N T A C H G
```

MAXIMILLION   DUBROVNIK   WATERLOOPLACE

LOLA   GUMBALL   CARRERAGT

GELLERTBATHS   KISHIMOTO

CAPRICE   COUNTACH

ICECREAMVAN   BIOFUEL   DAVE COURTNEY

DARYLHANNAH   RALLYRAID

SPECTRE   CUBANBROTHERS   SIBENIK

GENERAL LEE   ENZO

GUMBALL 3000 guess who

a)

b)

c)

d)

Belgium
Acoz

The cars park peacefully on display inside the castle walls

"Take a look outside!"

Chateau D'Acoz, located near Acoz not far from Brussels, was the first checkpoint in Europe, perfectly situated in order to give drivers a quick boost of caffeine and stock up on food before heading back out onto the road and navigating their way through the night across central Europe in their quest to reach Prague for breakfast.

Cars began arriving into the sleepy town of Acoz around Midnight, and to every Gumballers surprise, considering the time, the town and countryside lanes were awash with people. Alot of people! It was estimated that approximately 30,000 people came to see the cars arrive and spend a few hours, so many in fact that it nearly made it nearly impossible for the cars to actually reach the Chateau as the windy lanes were so busy with screaming fans that you could barely see the road, let alone signs to the checkpoint. Those that did make it to the Chateau checkpoint found a serene tranquillity after crossing the chateau's moat and parking inside the courtyard.

In 2006, Belgium once again plays host to a midnight checkpoint, this time however, the checkpoint is at an even more prestigious venue, Chateau de Beloeil, home to Belgium Prince de Ligne. This chateau has a moat all the way around, and from the reaction in 2005, this year we will certainly need it

FAN'TASTIC CROWDS

The crowds close in...

Pierce Brosnan must be lost!

Spot the Ferrari?

The end of the road?!

Who said the London Grand Prix can't happen!

Alex Roy lost for words!

Hummer chases Porsche GT!

An Austrian welcome!

Dubrovnick's main street Stradum grid-locked with fans!

Bridge after bridge for 3000 miles!

Waiting for the first car...

Vienna comes to a halt!

TECH SPEC

0-60 (mph): 4.4 secs
Max speed (mph): 175mph
Max power: 304bhp
Miles per gallon: 20mpg
Engine size: 2200cc
Cost new: £60,000
Total produced: 649
Modifications: Too many to list

STONKED IT!

Alex Roy

Ferenc Bekesi

In the words of Mark 'STONKED IT' Muss

Did anything break on the car?
On arriving to Prague our clutch was burned out from doing too many wheel spins. The only solution was to fly a Lotus mechanic and clutch from the UK and work throught the night. We were ready in time to start the next day.

What is the best way of getting off a speeding ticket?
My co-pilots Diplomatic ID!!

How did you get on with your co-driver? Any tensions?
After driving all night then no sleep and fixing the car thru the next night, on the way to Vienna we had a good old handbag fight!!!!

What was the best and/or most outrageous driving you saw?
No question my co-pilot Seamus 'Balkan Express' Conlan driving at nearly 300 km/h in the wet in Germany overtaking millions of dollars of cars who were running on slick tyres while we had special Dunlop rain tyres.

Did you get lost?
Only because our sat nav couldn't handle the speeds we were doing so we missed a few exits

What was your bar bill in Monaco?
Equivalent to the GDP of a small country.

Sum up your Gumball 3000 experience in one word? STONKING!!

V Max

Marks Prototype rear wing...

H 2 DCA

3ezer.com

Introducing co-driver
Seamus "Balkan Express "
Conolan

Jonathan Bushell

Mark and Maximillion
share the first dance!

Gumball My Ride

Pimp out your seats with snake skin!

Get your mates together

Check your flame-throwers work!

Campervan owner Dave Carrington had a plan. That was, to pimp up his 1963 Volkswagen Split-Screen 23 window Samba Campervan to eat up supercars for breakfast. And this is how he did it...

Fit a shift light for precision driving!

Add some chromes!

Fit a Porsche 911 engine!

Install a plasma screen and an x-box!

Add two bottles of nitros oxide!

Overtaking a Ferrari at speed!

Czech Republic
Praha

DC Shoes co-founder Damon Way crosses the finish line at the end of stage 1 in his custom Subaru Impreza WRX STi rally car!

Gumballers arrived deliriously tired into the Czech Republic's capital city of Prague, upon completing stage 1. Having driven just over 800 miles non-stop through the night all the way from London, only the hoardes of Czech Gumball fans cheering the cars in could keep the drivers awake long enough to park their car, and check in to the hotel Carlo IV, before getting some much needed sleep during the afternoon.

Although not known for missing a party, Gumballers awoke mere hours later raring to party again as Prague was alive with 'Gumball and Ice-hockey fever!' Adding to the atmosphere, that evening the countries ice-hockey national team also won the final of the World Championships against Canada. The city errupted as the final whistle blew, and Gumballers and ice hockey fans partied the night away in the town square!

31

Caprice 'n' Pepa

Push it, push it real good!

When Caprice Bourret ventured to England from Southern California she quickly became one of the most photographed women in the world, appearing on over 300 magazine covers across the globe. She was voted GQ Magazine's Woman of the Year and Maxim's International Woman of the Year three years running, and her pin-up calendar has been a top-selling international product for five consecutive years.

In March 2005, she joined Sandy Denton, Pepa of 80s hip hop group Salt N Pepa fame, and another past Gumballer, freestyle MX rider Carey Hart on the 5th season of the VH1 series The Surreal Life. One night live on air, after talking about sex (Salt N Pepa's best selling hit!) their conversation turned to Gumball and they called Maximillion from the house to ask if they could drive in the rally together. Max agreed, and the following month they were on the starting grid in their Porsche Turbo with Caprice at the wheel!

Caprice had the ride of her life!

A superbabe for a super rally!

Caprice gets wet with the guys at the party in Budapest!

DIABLO

1992

In June 1985, Automobili Lamborghini started thinking about a replacement for their legendary Countach. It would take the Lamborghini development team another five years to complete their new super car, the Diablo. The main directive for the Diablo was simple - its top speed had to be at least 200mph.

The name 'Diablo' was taken from a ferocious bull raised by a Spanish Duke. In 1869 the bull fought an epic battle with 'El Chicorro' in Madrid. Diablo the bull became legendary and it's name was deemed worthy enough to be used for the ferocious Lamborghini Diablo.

When a Spanish father and daughter team applied to do the 2005 Gumball in their 1992 Diablo with rainbow stripes, we knew they would make a colourful addition to the starting grid. Their reason for entering on the application form was they "intended to represent the gay community of Spain."

Roberto Brodolini

TECH SPEC

0-60 (mph): 4.5 secs
Max speed (mph): 197mph
Max power: 492bhp
Miles per gallon: 17mpg
Engine size: 5707cc
Cost new: £140,000
Total produced: 900
Modifications: Special Exhaust

David Lane

Tequilla Sunset

Musoll

A proud father and daughter pose
with their very own legendary bull!

Musoll

Max and Pere talking hairstyles
at the finish party in Monaco.

H2 VS

STATS ★★★★★★★★★★★★★★★

0-60MPH	**9.2 SECS**
MAX SPEED	**100 MPH**
MAX POWER	**340 BHP**
CAPACITY	**6000 CC**

LM002

★★★★★★★★★★★★★★★★★ STATS

0-60MPH	7.5 SECS
MAX SPEED	126 MPH
MAX POWER	455 BHP
CAPACITY	5500 CC

Fiona McLeod

Gumballers edge through the crowds looking for the carpark!!!?

Todays checkpoint en route to Budapest was at the Hofburg Imperial Palace in Vienna. An estimated 200,000 fans cheered in the 120 cars, lining the streets for over 5 miles, all asking for autographs from every Gumball driver, and even helping to push the overheating VW Porsche Campervan the last kilometre. This checkpoint was just insane. Gumball is BIG in Vienna!!!

39

SO HOW DO YOU GET TO RIDE WITH THE WILDEST RALLY IN THE WORLD? WHO IS THE THE ELUSIVE 'MAN WITH THE PLAN'? WILL HE ONE DAY COME FOR YOU? WHAT IF HE DOES AND YOU'RE IN THE LOO?..IN YOUR SHED?..OR SKATING IN THE X GAMES FINALS?

DON'T MISS... YOUR...

TICKET TO DRIVE

GUMBALL 3000

FEATURING
TONY 'BIRDMAN' HAWK
BAM MARGERA
INTRODUCING

CAPTAIN GUMBALL

SOMEWHERE OVER LA...

UH-OH! THIS AIN'T RIGHT- I ALWAYS LAND THIS ONE!

MAN I'M BORED!.. WHAT I NEED IS AN ADVENTURE!!

OW! WHAT'S THAT?!!

WOW! A 900 TO FACE-PLANT!

SLAM

TONY HAWK LONDON NOW!!

HMM! A GOLDEN GUMBALL? SOMETHING'S GOING ON HERE...

MEANWHILE, BY THE POOL

I'D BEST TALK TO BAM!!

CHILL OUT, DUDE!...

...JUST BECAUSE I PEED IN YOUR MOM'S STEAM IRON, DOESN'T MEAN I WOULD PUT CROC'S IN YOUR POOL!..

VIVA LA BAM

40

ON THE ROAD

Cars of all shapes and sizes do the Gumball. Some opt for speed, some for style, others 'bio-diesel' and the rest are just asking for trouble!

LOLA T70 MK3

As factory Fords, Ferraris and Porsches stamped their unforgettable presence on the world of endurance racing in the late 1960's and early 1970's, only one car gave privateers the chance to stand up to them - the British built Lola T70.

Powered by an enormous 6litre V8 with 1700lb of torque, it has a lightweight body, no windscreen, no speedo and no driver aids like traction control! It took such tremendous driving skill to get these brutes round the track, that so many racing enthusiasts believe the race series' these cars used to compete in were the greatest ever.

This beautiful, charismatic and super rare car is the only road legal Lola T70 in the world. It was restored and converted into this road going guise (complete with rear luggage rack) especially for the Gumball and driven by a Kiwi couple.

Questionably the rawest Gumball driving experience there has ever been!

Mai Ikuzawa

TECH SPEC

0-60 (mph): 4.0 secs
Max speed (mph): 185mph
Max power: 425bhp
Miles per gallon: 9mpg
Engine size: 6200cc
Cost new: £140,000
Total produced: 47
Modifications: Number plates!

David Harvey

Form follows function?!

Jonathan Bushell

A flies eye view!

"Girl Next Door?"
Kayleigh Pearson

This is Kayleigh Pearson, and guys if you've heard the name but are not quite familiar, then it may be because you don't recognise her with her clothes on! Kayleigh beat thousands of entrants to be named readers' favourite girl next door in FHM magazine, Britain's biggest-selling men's magazine.

Blonde, bubbly and cute as a button, Kayleigh took part in the 2005 rally for NUTS magazine, driving a 2005 Honda Civic Type R. Here's what she thought:

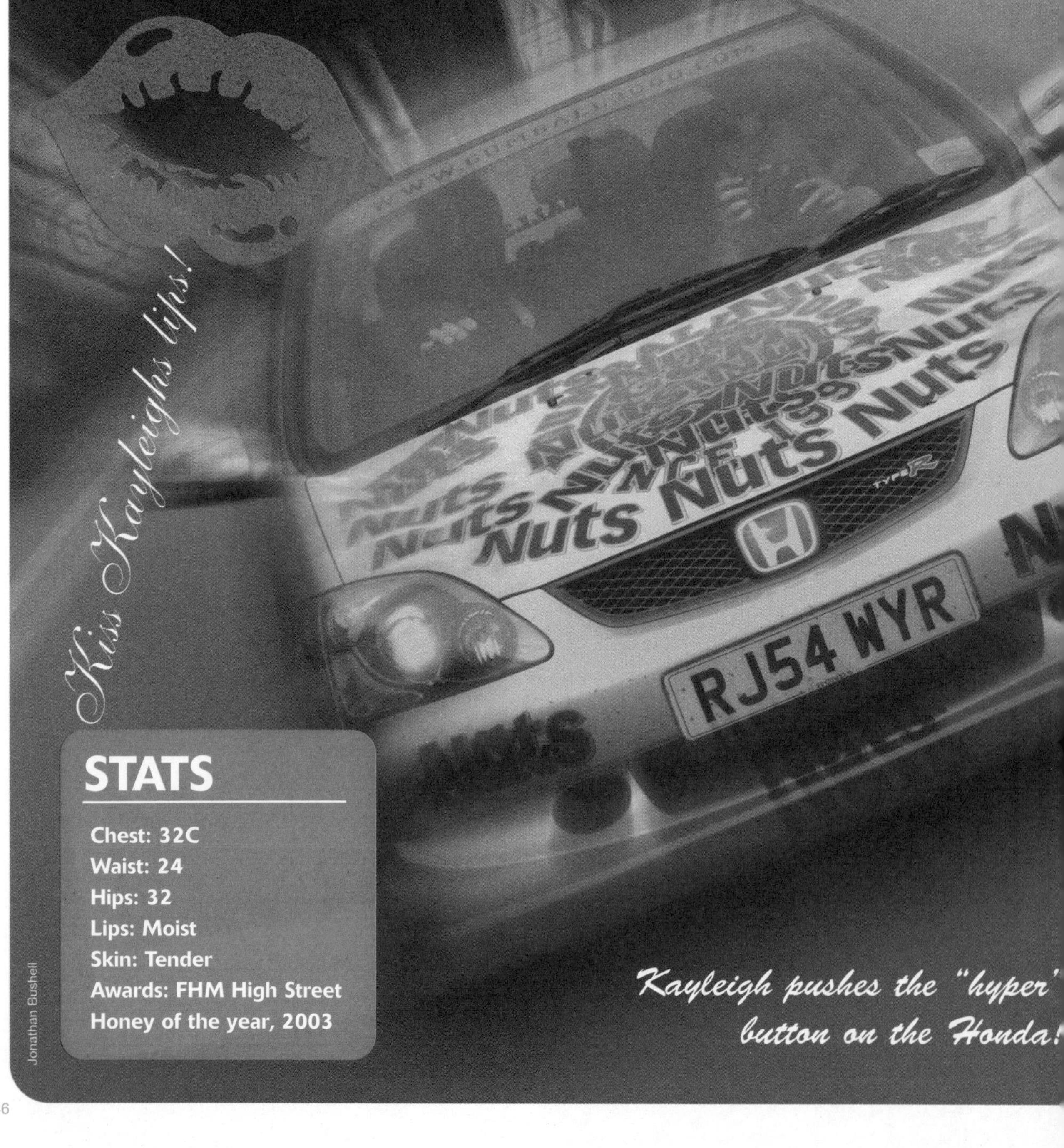

Kiss Kayleighs lips!

STATS

Chest: 32C
Waist: 24
Hips: 32
Lips: Moist
Skin: Tender
Awards: FHM High Street Honey of the year, 2003

Jonathan Bushell

Kayleigh pushes the "hyper" button on the Honda!

What is the best way of getting off a speeding ticket?
Got off two speeding tickets in Croatia by giving the police my autograph!

What was your best moment on the Gumball?
The whole thing, 7 days of pure adrenaline!

Did you do any driving on the rally?
No, I'd lost my license for speeding the day before we left!

Whats your favorite driving music?
My go faster God's Kitchen CD.

Sum up your Gumball experience in one word!
Magical!

Looking like the NUTS!

If only thats what the police really looked like!

Kayleigh gets to grips with their machinery

Kayleigh works her magic on the Croatian police

Gumball My Ride

Rally Raid UK was founded in 1999 by Paul Round following his participation in the famous Paris-Dakar Rally. Paul's first year proved to be a baptism by fire, being the only British entrant and very nearly the only English-speaker. Since then he has strived to help other Brits compete the Dakar and other rallies, and this year, he and co-driver Martin Coulson entered their first Gumball in their Paris-Dakar prepared Landrover/BMW hybrid. With a fuel tank large enough to cover nearly 2000 miles without stopping, this hybrid made an interesting match for those thirsty supercars.

Prepare yourself for sand storms!

Remove stock radio and CD player and fit an intercom!

48

Start by throwing away everything except the engine!

Don't forget to bring spare tyres!

Add 12" of suspension travel

Make a tubular steel roll cage at home!

Enter the Paris-Dakar as a warm up for Gumball!

Fit custom body!

Somewhere in the Sahara desert...!

Text and Photos, Martin Coulson

HOW TO JUMP LIKE

Maximillion and Johnny Knoxville have been friends for some years. As Johnny was starring in the Dukes of Hazzard movie Max decided to turn his Ferrari 550 LM into the General Lee...so they could practise jumping over rivers and canyons to get away from Boss Hogg!

You too can learn how to jump like the 'General Lee!' In 5 easy steps:

STEP 1

Find a broken bridge across a river, or simply build your own ramp.

STEP 2

Calculate how fast you need to drive to clear the river, or just guess if your maths is not that good.

STEP 3

Strap yourselves in the car, turn the engine on, drive slowly up to the ramp, take a look, then reverse to get a good run up.

..... THE DUKES!

STEP 4

Mentally prepare yourself, then floor it and hang onto that wheel with everything you've got!

STEP 5

When you get airborn after practise you'll pick your landing spot, but if its your first time, just scream..."YEEEEE HAWW!"

Croatia
Dubrovnik

The Sinclair C5 is parked comfortably atop the Porsche 911 of its owner, Crispin Sinclair, son of eccentric designer, Sir Clive Sinclair, on display in Dubrovnik's main street 'Stradun'.

The Croatian government welcomed the Gumball with open arms, creating a 'postage stamp' in commemoration of the rally coming to this amazing country, and making it a national holiday for the public to watch the cars race by!

On route from Budapest to Dubrovnik, a checkpoint was arranged in Croatia's National Park K.R.K.A in Sibernik beside a stunning waterfall. Serene and tranquil away from the constant roaring sound of their engines the Gumballers relaxed by the river in the afternoon sun. The drive then took the rally on the most stunning windy 'James Bond' style coastal roads before reaching the ancient city walls of Dubrovnik, where crowds of onlookers cheered each car home.

George Bernard Shaw was enchanted by this beautiful city: for him, it was paradise. Edward VIII and Mrs. Simpson's last trip abroad before they were married was to Dubrovnik. Prince Charles visited a few years ago and left captivated. In 2005 the GUMBALL came to town!!! Millions of people took to the streets to watch the amazing array of super and wacky cars arrive into this "jewel of the Adriatic".

The old town was completed in the 13th century and remains virtually unchanged to the present day. Tall ramparts surround it and there are only two entrances to the old town which lead to the Stradun, the city's promenade where the Gumball cars were allowed to park on display. Only presidents and the Pope have previously been given permission to drive here!
Dubrovnik has a remarkable history. An independent, merchant republic for 700 years (abolished by Napoleon in 1806), it traded with Turkey and India in the East and had trade representatives in Africa. It even had diplomatic relations with the English court in the middle ages. (There is a letter from Elizabeth I on display in the City Museum in Dubrovnik). Its status was such that powerful and rich Venice was envious of this Croatian-Slav city. However amazing this photograph looks, it still does not give justice to this dazzling place, which comes highly recommended from the Gumball, why not come and see it with your own eyes!

Greetings from Italy

Roberto Brodolini

Check out the arse on that!!

TECH SPEC

0-60 (mph): 4.9 secs
Max speed (mph): 183mph
Max power: 455bhp
Miles per gallon: 16mpg
Engine size: 5167cc
Cost new: £100,000 (1989)
Total produced: 657
Modifications: Sports Exhaust

The drivers view

All text Julian Gillet

I have owned the earliest Diablo, the final 6 litre Diablo and a Murcielago, however, the Countach sits at the top for the driving experience. This was the last car designed by Ferrucio Lamborghini and arguably this is where the modern supercars started.

The driving position on the Countach is sharply offset to the left to accomodate the large wheel arch which takes up alot of the room where the pedals are, this leaves for a very narrow accelerator and it takes practice (and small shoes) not to hit two pedals at a time.The seats are very comfortable however and although entering the car can be awkward, interior space is fine if you are less than 6ft. Reversing needs to be done sat on the sill looking over the back of the car and rear visibility is at best limited - but open the engine bay and you see the point with the V12 supported by the largest rear tyres fitted to any production car at 345 cms. Oh and watch the clutch, slip this and kiss goodbye to £5,000.

This Countach was bought purely for the Gumball, and the driving experience was simply incredible. We didn't listen to music once – just the sound of the V12 – and yes it was comfortable – unforgettable….

Not many expected the Countach to make it especially as it had covered only 5000 miles from new and had hardly been used in the previous ten years. A progressive electrical fault saw the air-conditioning give up in Austria and the windscreen wipers pack up just before Rome (during torrential rain) but the mechanicals were faultless and we did make it to Monaco. The electrics did give up on the journey home at Marseilles where it was treated to a trip home on the back of a trailer.

How to arrive in style

Jonathan Bushell

At 4:00pm on the day of the rally I was at a friends wedding in Swindon with the rally due to start at 6:00pm. I chartered a helicopter for exactly 4:30pm when the ceremony finished and was in the air 5 minutes later. I landed at Battersea at 5:20pm where a motorbike was waiting – the rider managed to cover the six miles in no time filtering through heavy traffic to deliver me at the start for 5:30pm where my co-driver Ben was waiting in the car ready to go – now that's how to start the Gumball!!

DC SUBARUS

2005 Subaru Impreza WRX STi

Team DC...

For 2005, DC shoes stepped up its involvement and became a main sponsor, sending a squad of DC drivers to enter the rally, including a pro skateboarder, Rob Dyrdek and "bodyguard" Big Black in one car, DC President Ken Block and his wife Lucy in another, and DC Executive Vice President Damon Way and his wife Suzie in a third. The DC Subarus were amongst the most 'eye-catching' cars in the rally, even among $500,000+ super-exotics, out performing many, putting out 450bhp, and hitting top speeds of 180mph.

The cars were custom created over a six month period, and they are street versions of Vermont Sportscars competition rally cars, and built upon the Subaru WRX STi's durability and speed with tons of Gumball-specific modifications, complete with TV, DVD, ipod cradles, custom safety gear, and each car featured a unique camouflage graphic!!!!

TECH SPEC

0-60 (mph): 4.5 secs
Max speed (mph): 180mph
Max power: 426bhp
Miles per gallon: 14mpg
Engine size: 2500cc
Cost new: £30,000 - B4 mods!
Total produced: 3, one offs!
Modifications: Too many

WIN

Roberto Brodol

Big Black models the new
Dyrdek Backpack

"We tortured these cars", said Ken!!!

The cars were capable of
180mph, but the speedo only
went to 160mph!

Team DC unwind at the
Gumball finish party Monaco
2005

Dave Courtney O.B.E

He thought he had seen it all until he did the Gumball 3000

Dave Courtney is one of London's best known former gangsters - in his time his vast amount of criminal contacts have led to him being dubbed the "Yellow Pages of Crime". On the darker side he's been shot and stabbed and has had to kill to stay alive. As the "heir to the Krays", Courtney was also the basis for Vinnie Jones' character in the movie Lock, Stock and Two Smoking Barrels. The former debt collector looks an evil b**tard, in fact he is an evil b**tard (if you wrong him), but Dave has now moved to a legitimate life of white Rolls Royces, castle walls around his house, his own graveyard headstone and even 2 HUGE eyes painted on his roof to let the police know, he is watching them too!

This year was Dave's first Gumball, driving a mean looking 2004 Ford F150 SVT Lightning, pimped up to the max, with his mate Andy. Here's what he thought...

Dan Anslow

care to pull over?

Career highlights:
14 not-guilty verdicts.

What was your top speed?
173mph - with nos!!

How much did you spend on fuel and speeding tickets?
Just the 7 speeding tickets with three and a half grands worth of fuel.

What is the best way of getting off a speeding ticket?
Put your foot down and don't stop!

What was your best moment on the Gumball?
Diving off the top of the boat into the sea at the finish party, it was at least a 100ft drop, honest guv!!

Were you pushed or did you jump off the boat in Monaco?
I jumped although Maximillion was suspiciously close!

What was your favourite driving music?
Elvis Presley. Jail bird rock!

What was your bar bill in Monaco?
Didn't pay it!

Do you always pack a piece?
Knuckleduster! One shot with it and your gone!

Do you think Maximillion would make a good gangster?
I thought he was one!

Were you pleased with your award?
I was well chuffed about the medal and I now have it hanging on my front wall!

Sum up your Gumball 3000 experience in one word.
Unforgettable.

The Dave Courtney

Dan Anslow

Courtney marks his man, 'nuff said'

stretcn Hummer

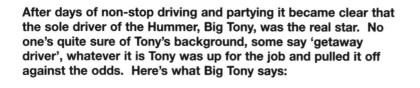

After days of non-stop driving and partying it became clear that the sole driver of the Hummer, Big Tony, was the real star. No one's quite sure of Tony's background, some say 'getaway driver', whatever it is Tony was up for the job and pulled it off against the odds. Here's what Big Tony says:

What would be your dream Gumball car?
A Delorean, I'd do the parties twice!

How much did you spend on fuel and speeding tickets?
I never got caught speeding but I done close to 3 grand in juice.

What car were you most envious of on the rally?
Bez's van because whenever I passed them they were always smiling!

Who from history would be your dream gumball co-pilot?
Amy Johnson, we'd fly!

What was your best moment on the Gumball?
Crossing the finish line. After 3000 miles of hard driving and even harder partying, with the end of the trip in sight the Monte Carlo police seemed intent on not letting me get through but I was having none of it.

The last three corners was a nightmare. It took me one and a half hours to get round them. The police were shouting and screaming that I would not do it, at least thats wot I think they were saying! We had to move the backs of yachts, a concrete flower bed and even lift a car out of the way but I wasn't going to let the last 50 yards beat me.

I was finally knicked for obstruction and escorted out of Monaco by 6 police bikes, but that didn't matter 'cos I'd done it!

What was your favorite driving music?
Kym (Mazelle) and the Cuban Brothers jamming in the back!

Did you get lost?
Yeah, I couldn't find my cabin after the finish party!

Sum up your Gumball experience in one word.
Insane!

Big Ton

Fine gambling company 888.com were an official sponsor of the 2005
ally and entered their own Stretch Hummer for larger than life presence.
he Hummer was home and party room for the Cuban Brothers: Miguel,
lemente, Archerio and Kym Mazelle from Soul II Soul.

Fiona McLeod

Soul Diva Kym Mazelle, Clemente
and Presenter Ed Leigh

Simon Jones

The Cubans Scottish
relatives!

Simon Jones

Meet Archerio- he is my
brother and also my cousin

Gumball My Ride

Style guru Diane Pernet shades herself from fashion!

Mark Eley is one of the two designers behind the fashion label Eley Kishimoto. He and his wife Wakako Kishimoto like to describe themselves as surface painters. Mark and his co-driver Jason Maclean drove a Volkswagen Golf GTI, customising the interior and bodywork in his own unmistakable style.

VW supported the entry, sending a full support crew of mechanics, stylists, hairdressers, cameramen, a helicopter, and they even had their own dedicated bonnet polishers!

Another glamorous road side 'truck stop' photoshoot!

Jason checks the steering

Night vision shades, check!

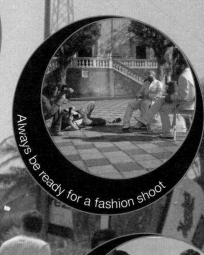

Always be ready for a fashion shoot

Head buffing is essential

Only allow supermodels to polish your bonnet!

Bring your own personal barber!

Sicilia Taormina

A Ferrari Enzo and 550 LM park proudly on the town square, in honour to the man himself. Enzo Ferrari took part in the Targa Florio in 1919 driving a Lancia in his first major race.

Having driven across mainland Italy from Bari, Gumballers took a ferry to Sicily and drove on the windy coastal roads to reach the medieval town of Taormina in the North East, home to the Godfather and the 'Targa Florio' road race. The famous 'Targa Florio' began life in 1906 not too dissimilar to the origins of the 'Gumball 3000'. The race was created in 1906 by the wealthy pioneer race driver and automobile enthusiast, Vincenzo Florio, who started it after purchasing a 'motor car' whilst travelling in Paris. The new contraption caused quite a sensation as it was unloaded onto the dock in Sicily. Unfortunately it stayed there due to the fact that there was not any gasoline available in all of Sicily! Urgent cables to Paris finally brought a shipment of the precious fuel. After the initial thrill of driving his new toy began to wear off he decided to invite his wealthy friends from around Europe and have a race. It soon became known as one of the toughest competitions in Europe, covering 277 miles through multiple hairpin curves on treacherous mountain roads, at heights where severe changes in climate frequently occurred. By the mid-1920s, the Targa Florio had become one of Europe's most important races, as neither the 24 Hours of Le Mans nor the Mille Miglia had been established yet; although much like the Gumball, the 'Targa Florio' was not so much a 'race' as it was an ordeal!

Over the years, the greats of Grand Prix racing and Formula One such as Argentina's Juan Manuel Fangio and Britain's Stirling Moss came to challenge Italian champions, Tazio Nuvolari, and Alfieri Maserati. Due to the long track, drivers practised in the week before the race in public traffic, often with their race cars fitted with license plates. After winning the race several times, Porsche named the convertible version of the 911 after the Targa. The name of the car with the large roll bar was a wise choice, as targa means shield. Due to safety concerns, the last real Targa Florio as an international professional race was run in 1973. In that year, a Porsche 911 won again as the prototypes suffered crashes or other troubles!

Driving slightly less hard or competitive, after arriving in Taormina the Gumballers partied the night away at the Grand Hotel Timeo, overlooking the sea on one side, and the mighty Mount Etna, Europe's largest active Volcano on the other. Al Pacino's famous wedding scene from Francis Ford Coppola's first Godfather movie was filmed here, and in 2002, the venue also played host to the wedding of Gumball bosses, Maximillion & Julie!

Auto Magazin

A rare British sporstcar, the Spectre R42

Sahle

The Enzo, centre of attent...

Nick Taft

The 2005 Farboud GT looks utterly outrageous on public roads!

Fiona McLeod

The IMB Roadcars supercar. Bet you've never seen this before!

Judit Musol

2005 McLaren Mercedes SLR, is this 'Batmans' new car?

"I'll have the Enzo than...

Take your pick...

It must be James Bond at the wheel of this Aston!

A 2005 Porsche Carrera GT in 'Bananaman yellow!'

2005 Pagani Zonda. Absolute supercar heaven!

Probably the most popular 'pin-up' in the world!

A 1992 Lamborghini Diablo loud in both colour and noise!

1989 Ferrari F40 and 2004 Ferrari Enzo sit on the roadside waiting for the rest of the pack to catch up......!!!

Ice Cream Van

The ice-cream siren tune of Green sleeves was allegedly written by King Henry VII

THE STORY OF THE SHOE!

In typical Gumball fashion, after a 'bust-up' with his other half en route to Budapest, a right shoe was ditched on the roadside. Undeterred, the shoe hitched with other Gumballers for the rest of the 3000 miles, determined to catch up with his partner. Upon reaching Monaco, their soles met across the dance floor, and once again they became a pair!

mine, all mine...

Hello, is there anybody th

"Who has the flake?"

GI Joe was happy with the days sales!

Carrying the mantle for all vehicles slow and eccentric that take part in the Gumball, like the Gumball winning Citroen 2CV in 2004, this year the ice cream van caused the biggest stir, and against all odds made it to the finish line despite breaking down several times, getting the shakes at above 50mph, and managing a top speed of about 15 mph up hills!

It's crew were absolutely eccentric, but there's method behind their madness. They have produced a movie called G.I. Jesus about the war in Iraq (safe to say they're not supporters), hence the desert camo look. The film focuses on a Mexican's quandry of whether to fight for the US in Iraq in return for a Green card. The reason director Matthew Devlen chose an ice cream van was to highlight Bush's policies that push kids towards the military. (Huummm!)

This particular 'ice-cream' van was borrowed from an 'ice-cream' man in Kent just the day before the rally started, and everybody laughed when it turned up on the starting rid, complete with full stock of ice-cream.

No one thought it would make it to the finish in Monaco, and it would appear that even the Monegasque Police were out to stop them, proclaiming that 'Ice-Cream' vans are "banned" in the Principality. Not sure about Prince Alberts reasoning for that rule, the kids have no clue what they're missing!

However, intrepid adventurer, Matthew and his co-driver Kimberley Green managed to complete the entire rally serving 'melted' ice-cream and playing 'Green sleeves' ice-cream jingle at every opportunity.

The day after the rally finished, the van's engine blew up 20 minutes outside Calais on its return to the UK, but determined to not go to the 'ice-cream' van graveyard, with a new engine fitted it is now back on the scene, serving 'ice-cream' to a village near you, if you live in Kent, that is!

And for the main...

whats that smell?

The shoe idea didn't have legs on it!

All shoe photos Matt Devlen

Daryl & Tina

Daryl 'Bio Diesel' Hannah!

Android, Mermaid, Assassin... this 5' 10" blonde beauty, with the haunting blue-green eyes, hit the big screen in 1982 in the role of the acrobatic, beautiful replicant Pris in Blade Runner. Showing her versatility, from there she portrayed a mermaid in the zany comedy Splash, and teamed up with Julia Roberts in the romantic comedy Steel Magnolias. Of Daryl's most recent roles, she is best-known for the one-eyed assassin Elle Driver in Kill Bill: Volumes I and II, directed by Quentin Tarantino.

Good friends with Tina, they teamed up to take part in the Gumball together, however as a keen environmentalist Daryl had one condition, insisting that their car runs only using 100% bio-diesel. For many years Daryl has lived simply using solar power, living in teepees and utilizing the best green building materials and practises in the construction of her modest and rustic home. Daryl has been involved in the bio-diesel movement for many years and has educated thousands of people through her appearances on the Tonight Show and Howard Stern.

Not many Gumballers know that any diesel engine can use bio-diesel without any modifications, and Daryl was keen to show the worlds media that bio-diesel rules! Not only is it helping to save the environment, but it's also way cheaper than dirty diesel!

Their Pink bio-diesel camouflage Range Rover edges its way through the Austrian crowds

70

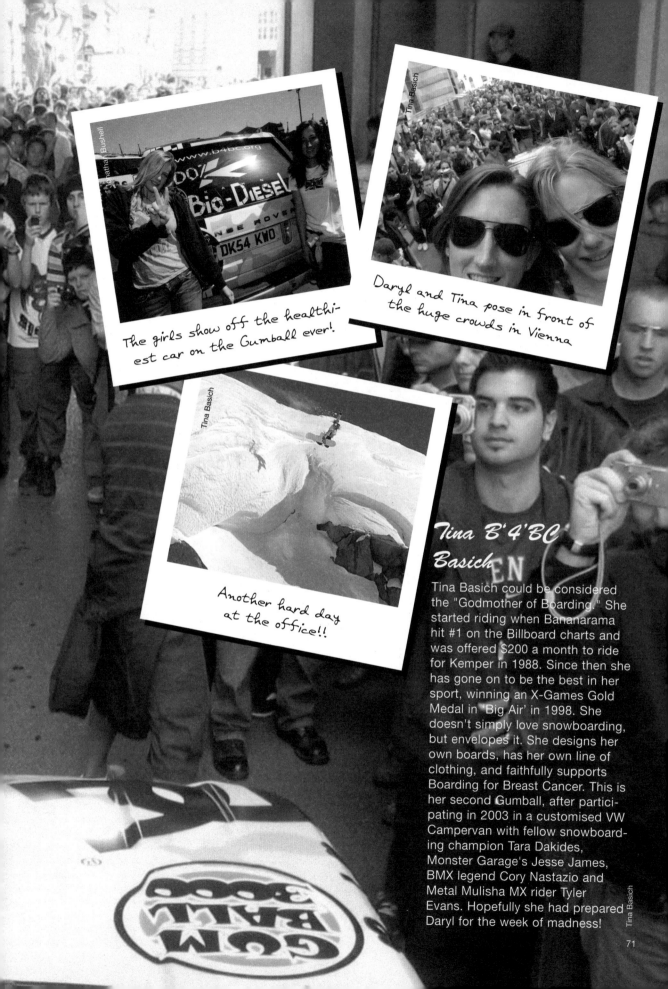

Jonathan Bushell

The girls show off the healthiest car on the Gumball ever!

Tina Basich

Daryl and Tina pose in front of the huge crowds in Vienna

Tina Basich

Another hard day at the office!!

Tina B'4'BC Basich

Tina Basich could be considered the "Godmother of Boarding." She started riding when Bananarama hit #1 on the Billboard charts and was offered $200 a month to ride for Kemper in 1988. Since then she has gone on to be the best in her sport, winning an X-Games Gold Medal in 'Big Air' in 1998. She doesn't simply love snowboarding, but envelopes it. She designs her own boards, has her own line of clothing, and faithfully supports Boarding for Breast Cancer. This is her second Gumball, after participating in 2003 in a customised VW Campervan with fellow snowboarding champion Tara Dakides, Monster Garage's Jesse James, BMX legend Cory Nastazio and Metal Mulisha MX rider Tyler Evans. Hopefully she had prepared Daryl for the week of madness!

Tina Basich

Italy
Roma

The drive to Rome was a real test of the drivers' skills of prowess and endurance, and unfortunately it took its toll on some of the cars. Like day five of the 2004 rally through Morocco, cars were expiring left right and centre. The 1970s Buick split its radiator, Richie Warren's 1970 Dodge Challenger left its sump on the ferry coming back to mainland from Sicily, and a sudden but torrential down pour, saw a 355 Ferrari, Porsche GT and Lamborghini Murcielago spinning pirouettes on the Autostrada.

Miraculously, almost no damage was done and the robust Porsche was gaffer taped up to continue on the rally, however the Lamborghini Murcielago wasn't so lucky...the central reservation left a not so beautiful modification along its side. The car was only 8 days old, and needless to say, the driver was not happy; however he quickly managed to rent a car and somehow managed to reach Rome early evening!

Spirit of the Gumball winner from 2003, Alex Roy also proved his legendary status once again on this stage by getting to the Sicilian ferry port by 8:25am and cordoning it off with 'Gumball' police tape. He then sailed alone on a ferry to mainland Italy and "cruised at 8/10ths" towards Rome, sirens and lights on continuously. Midway to Rome the M5 Polizei car had it's lead threatened by a blue Porsche Turbo being driven brilliantly by Spencer Bourne. A 90-minute battle ensued taking the cars all the way into Rome, with the Porsche overtaking on clear roads and Alex using his sirens to take the lead when traffic built up. Eventually the Porsche slipped back due to Spencer's "poor toll booth strategy" and "poor GPS strategy" (wrong turn) leaving the delighted cops claiming another victory!

Cars arrive into Piazza della Republica, greeted by crowds and a red carpet fanfare for the premiere of the new Star Wars film, Episode III: Revenge of the Sith.

Jonathan Bushell

73

2004
Lamborghini Gallardo:
Team Polizia

TECH SPEC

0-60 (mph): 4.2 secs
Max speed (mph): 205mph
Max power: 492bhp
Miles per gallon: 14mpg
Engine size: 4961cc
Cost new: £130,000
Total produced: 1490
Modifications: Polizia Wrap

Yorgo Tloupas

Let me buy you a donut officer...

Q&A with Simon Jones, Team Polizia

What was your top speed? 205mph
Did anything break on the car?
The radar detector when the French police stamped on it.
Any special modifications?
The laser jammers which the police couldn't find!
How much did you spend on fuel and speeding tickets?
£800 fuel / 1500 euro on tickets.
What is the best way of getting off a speeding ticket?
Let the police sit in the car and take a photo.
What was the most outrageous thing you did on the rally?
Overtook an Italian police car on the hard shoulder.

Tell me another little story that springs to mind about your Gumball experience?
We got caught in a speed trap in Austria and were told that the speed limit was only 80kph – we were doing 270kph! Thinking we were in big trouble, the policeman told us that we were to give him 500 euro as a 'special gift' and then he wanted his photo taken with his mobile phone. He then told us to drive off and show him what the car could do! Obviously we obliged!.
What, to you, is the Spirit of the Gumball?
Harmlessly breaking a few laws and having a lot of fun!
Sum up your Gumball 3000 experience in one word? Mint!

Team Jakera

Team Jakera, made up of; the 3 Patterson brothe[rs]
Tim, Chris and Frankie (ex-guitarist from rock gr[oup]
The Darkness), and friends Seamus, Neil and
Christian, clubbed together to buy two cars for
$3,000 a week before the rally, just to prove that [they]
can do the Gumball in style without a $100,000 c[ar].
This is how their adventure panned out....

Name: Chris Patterson.
Car driven in Gumball? 1966 GTO convertible.
How did it perform? Like a rock star.
Did anything break on the car? Just the engine.
What car were you most envious of on the rally?
The stretch hummer, what a party going on in there!
**How much did you spend on fuel and speeding
tickets?** $2000 on fuel and $100 on a ticket for going
through a red light.
Any tensions? Only in Prague, when we temporarily
ran out of herbal tea.
**What was the best and/or most outrageous driving
you saw?** My big brother Tim, in his Buick. I was actu-
ally relieved when he couldn't drive it any more after he
wrote it off!
What's your daily ride? My girlfriend, Ada.
**What was the most outrageous thing you did on the
rally?** Out running the Hungarian mafia.
**Who from history would be your dream Gumball co-
driver?** Dick Van Dyke.
**Tell me a story that springs to mind about your
Gumball experience?** Buying half a kilo of oregano in
Prague.   Say no more!!
Sum up your Gumball 3000 experience in one word.
Supercalifradulisticexpialidocious.

Name: Tim 'HotRod' Poullain-Patterson.
Career highlights: 'Most Promising Jazz Trumpet
Player' - Edinburgh Festival 1984
Car driven in Gumball? Buick Riviera GS 1970.
What was your top speed? Speedometer didn't wo[rk]
Did anything break on the car? Where do i
start...(see pic)
What car were you most envious of on the rally?
Dodge Challenger 440 R/T -what a sound system!
What is the best way of getting off a speeding tick[et?]
Don cloak of invisibility
Any tensions? Slight pain in Seamus's leg when I
crashed the car... otherwise we're both fine thanks.
What was the best and/or most outrageous drivi[ng]
you saw? Seamus driving like a maniac on the way [to]
the ferry in Dubrovnik - we were late, it was night tim[e]
and the headlights didn't work...
Any tips on how to stay stylish on the Gumball?
Bring a bar of soap
What was your best moment on the Gumball?
Departing London in a blaze of smoke and rubber.
What, to you, is the Spirit of the Gumball? Vodka
Martini with a lemon twist.
Sum up your Gumball 3000 experience.
Life-affirming.

Main image Dan Anslow, Video footage Team Jake[ra]

If you can't join them....
Beat them!

All text Chris Patterson

Basically, we snuck out of Sicily and drove down to the harbour to get the 1am ferry which would take us to within two hours drive of Rome. With seconds to spare we managed to get onto the ferry and after another sleepless night drinking the ferry bar dry, we arrived back on terra firma, and were delighted to see that Rome was only 200km away! It was only 8 a.m so we had a good chance of arriving by midday, and possibly even coming in first if we pushed the GTO, so I put my foot down, turned up the music, and hoped for the best... sure enough she overheated and we had to stop and let her cool down! We were soon underway and were doing well with only 20 km to Rome before she over heated again and we had to stop. It was around 11 am and we realised that we still had a good chance of getting to Rome first, so we all prayed over the engine and begged her to start up again, and sure enough she did!

Now we were into the home straight and all was looking good until the Russian Roller went flying past us, we all stood up and gave them the finger, but then realised that this was not so bad, maybe we were not going to be first, but we were at least on the right road... probably! We came in an amazing 7th place. Everyone wanted to know how we had managed to beat all the super cars, steam was pouring out of our engine and she sounded awful, so I told the reporters that we drove the GTO as fast as we could all the way from Sicily because we were determined to win, but in the process we had blown the engine. So the next day I rented a truck to take us to the French border where I planned to drive the car the last leg into Monaco for a triumphant finish.

Simon Jones

Photo Neil Fox. Illustration Tim Hutton

Get your hands off my woman!

ガンボール3000 🇯🇵
生沢徹＆生沢舞
父娘の風狂レース参戦記

🇯🇵 イクザワ マイ ＋A
MAI IKUZAWA ＋A
✚ ジョイ ジュリア ＋O
JULIA JOY ＋O

AUTO SPORT-6

Tetsu Ikuzawa
Legendary Japanese racing driver from 1963 - 1977

Mai Ikuzawa
Tetsu's only daughter, Mai, grew-up watching her father race. 'Daddy, I want to do the Gumball Rally!', Tetsu had no choice but to make some important calls...

Mai & Julia
Two girls, one mission, 3,000 miles in six days.

Team Ikuzawa
The first official Japanese entry for the Gumball Rally with its motorsports crew and support vehicle.

Starting Grid
Tetsu debriefs Jenson Button and Maximillion Cooper to look after his daughter!

Customised Lexus SC430
Somewhere lost in Belgium...

6am towards Prague
Julia catches up on her beauty sleep. The passenger seat becomes your bed for the next five days.

Breakdown
Lost, tired, hungry...and not even reached the first check-point.

Check-in Prague
The girls packed just the bare essentials.

Team Ikuzawa Mechanics
Kanazawa-san ends up fixing other cars and walking sticks as Ikuzawa-spec Lexus SC430 proves its Japanese reliability.

NAME
Mai Ikuzawa
Julia Joy

NATIONALITY
MI: Japanese
JJ: Danish

HOME TOWN
MI: London, Tokyo

WHATS YOUR JOB
MI: CEO of BOW WOW
bowwowlondon.com

JJ: Creative Director of Camilla and Julia

CAR DRIVEN IN GUMBALL?
Custom Lexus SC430

HOW DID YOUR CAR PERFORM IN THE GUMBALL?
With grace and sophistication - less said for the drivers.

DID ANYTHING BREAK ON THE CAR?
Mai broke down in Rome.

ANY SPECIAL MODIFICATIONS, IF SO HOW MUCH?
8POT ceramic reinforced aluminium brake-system supplied by Akebono, wheels supplied by RAYS Engineering, tyres supplied by Dunlop, undercar lighting and suspension lighting supplied by Varad, all other

IF YOU KNOW THEM, PLEASE LET US KNOW THE FOLLOWING STATS FROM YOUR CAR:
Max Speed · 155mph
0-60 · 6.2secs
Max Power · 282BHP
Miles per Gallon · 23.5mpg
Engine Capacity · 4293cc
Cost · £55,000 basic

WHAT WOULD BE YOUR DREAM GUMBALL CAR?
Nissan Skyline GTR, Suzuki LC, Honda NSX, Honda WOW.

WHAT IS THE BEST WAY OF GETTING OFF A SPEEDING TICKET?
Use support car as a decoy. After a couple of days on the rally, 2 sweaty Japanese men

Under Cover
FIA regulated AWS Nomex racesuits had to come off in the Croatian sun.

Cruising to Rome
Driving with Team Eley Kishimoto who also took it very seriously.

Polizia
Team Ikuzawa gets to test drive the ultimate Italian get-away car.

WWW.BOWWOWLONDON.COM

日本製
MADE
IN JAPAN

Team Ikuzawa
Choice of Racing Enthusiasts

Casino Square
Proud Daddy Ikuzawa greets the exhausted drivers with a magnum of Champagne at Hotel Metropole.

Monaco F1 Grandprix
Team Ikuzawa enjoys a lap of honour for the Japanese media.

So close yet so far...
Monaco was not so welcoming.

WHAT'S YOUR DAILY RIDE?
MI: 'PINKU' - a hot pink customised Toyota Celica import.
JJ: Ford Mustang Convertible with ghetto silver cobra locks.

WHAT'S YOUR FAVORITE CAR-SCENE IN A MOVIE?
'Jackie Stewart: Weekend of a Champion' by Roman Polanski. ★★★★★

WHAT WAS THE MOST OUTRAGEOUS THING YOU DID ON THE RALLY?
Sleep.

ANY TIPS ON HOW TO STAY STYLISH ON THE GUMBALL?
Unload the jerry-cans and spare wheels in the support car and refill it with cocktail dresses shipped directly en route from Celux, Tokyo.

WHAT WAS YOUR WORST MOMENT ON THE GUMBALL?
Doing an additional 500 miles getting lost in Belgium with a 6ft 4 camera man squeezed in the tiny rear seats doing an interview of how we are getting on!!?

WHAT WAS YOUR FAVOURITE DRIVING MUSIC?
J-Pop.

WHAT WAS YOUR BEST MOMENT ON THE GUMBALL?
Richie, Ben, Mark, Jason, Diane, Linda, Yuni, Matt, Karta, Yorgo, Fiona, Ezra, Dicky, Damian... It was like summer camp as it should have been.

DID YOU GET LOST?
Yes. And sadly, it was well-documented on the official Gumball TV series this year.

WHAT, TO YOU, IS THE SPIRIT OF THE GUMBALL?
Convincing our ex-racing driver father that the Gumball Rally is a world-class motoring event. Then getting him to supply you with a fully-customised rally car, a support car, his team mechanics, uniform, sponsors and pocket money.

SUM UP YOUR GUMBALL 3000 EXPERIENCE IN ONE WORD?
Banzai.

2005 ROLLS ROYCE PHANTOM

Ron Jones

This stately car was driven by Ezra Chapman, Richard Blackburn and Damian Williams.

How did your car perform in the Gumball?
Awesome... the most luxurious and chic car on the planet.

Out of 10 what score would you give your car on the Gumball?
9 out of 10 (see next question).

What was your top speed?
150mph (restricted unfortunately).

Did anything break on the car?
Apart from feeling personally broken we only had a few scathes the flying lady on the front jammed up and one of the umbrellas in the door well broke.

Any special modifications?
Rolls Royce removed the front indicator repeaters on the wings and installed some flag masts to help personalize her for us. Our pirate flags got big respect on the road.

How much did you spend on fuel and speeding tickets?
Lots on fuel and Richard lost his license in Hungary picking up a cool 700Euro on the spot fine.

How did you get on with your co-

N6

Nick Taft

TECH SPEC

0-60 (mph): 5.5 secs
Max speed (mph): 150mph
Max power: 453bhp
Miles per gallon: 8mpg
Engine size: 6000cc
Cost new: £260,000
Total produced: N/A
Modifications: Pirate flags

Jonathan Bushell

Pirates of the Mediterranean?

What was your best moment on the Gumball?
Cruising the brand new and most beautiful Croatian motorways for hours on end, flat out!

What was your favourite driving music?
Timo Mass.

Did you get lost?
Didn't everybody?

What was your bar bill in Monaco?
Purposely avoided looking.

Sum up your Gumball 3000 experience in one word.
blaGlum!

UM

sometimes only inches from killing each other, and thats just before getting to the first checkpoint!

What was the most outrageous thing you did on the rally?
Enter.

Any tips on how to stay stylish on the Gumball?
Remember - comfort before fashion.

drivers?
We were a team of 3 and there were plenty of tensions,

Monaco
Monte Carlo

*An Enzo crosses the finish line in
Casino Square to a sea of onlookers!*

For over 50 years the Monaco Grand Prix has been regarded as the most prestigious motor race in the world, and the seductiveness of Monte-Carlo during the Grand Prix of Monaco week is like no other. Monaco is where high rollers come to experience motor racing, so where else could the 2005 'Gumball 3000' Rally finish, but in Monaco's prestigious Casino Square.

The drive from Rome to Monte Carlo was a long stretch, and although the Gumballers were near the end of the rally, they weren't letting up whatsoever and the day was again full of drama. After leading the pack for most of the 3000 miles, even the McLaren Mercedes of gentleman racing driver Oliver Morley suffered a technical problem, with a flat tyre just outside Monaco, allowing Monegasque resident Gregorio Tunon to cruise past in his stealthy 2004 AMG CLK DTM Mercedes to arrive first into Casino Square.

After crossing the finish line and soaking up the sprayed champagne, exhausted and elated drivers boarded the 'Gumball' luxury cruise ship in the harbour ready for another 'all-nighter', dancing the night away as the Cuban Brothers lit up the dance floor!

The following day, Gumballers relaxed with their cocktails by the pool, watching (and listening) to the deafening sounds of F1 qualifying, preparing themselves for the evenings Awards ceremony that took place on the ship that night.

AWARDS
With your host Maximillion Cooper

Jonathan Bushell

Gumball Enthusiast Award

This award went to Mark Muss for impeccable preparation, always running at the front and overcoming a string of car troubles.

Jonathan Bushell

Tough Guys Award

Original gangster Dave Courtney and his co-Andy Gardener aptly won the award for kee all the entrants in check.

Jonathan Bushell

Gumball Bling Award

Dave Carrington and friends scooped this award for entering their pimped out VW Camper van.

Jonathan Bushell

Unity VIP Quote of the Rally

Big Black to a waiter in Monaco:
"Don't tell me the price I'm f@£%ing rich!"

Jonathan Bushell

A Special Award

Went to the two (nameless) guys who managed to wreck the engine on one car and write another off. Total bill £400,000!

Jonathan Bushell

Co-Pilot Navigation award

Matt Devlen and Co. creamed the oppposition to win this award for managing to get their 40mph Ice Cream van round the whole event.

Jonathan Bushell

Gumball Davida Style Award

Team Jakera for their unrelenting flow of cool outfits during the event and always wearing smiles no matter what!

Jonathan Bushell

Best Driver Award

Soul Diva Kym Mazelle aptly won this award for incredibly managing to complete four Gumballs without ever doing any driving!

Jonathan Bushell

Meguiars Cleanest Car Award

Fashion guru Mark Eley of Eley Kishimoto cleaned up with this award thanks to his crew of beautiful people polishing his car at every opportunity.

Fiona Mcleod

DC Shoes Lifetime Award

Karta Healy took this award away with him because he has competed in every Gumball since 1999!

Spirit of the Gumball

Team 76:
1990 Caterham Super 7

Is that an engine???!!!

Nuts

0590A

Simon Jones

Always the centre of attention!

Jonathan Bushell

Sue Bellarby and Kathryn Huddart with past winner Alex Roy

Winners of The Spirit of the Gumball Award Goes to "Team 76" Sue Bellarby and Kathryn Huddart driving their 1990 Caterham Super 7!

Each year the grand finale of the award ceremony is the coveted 'Spirit of the Gumball Award'. This year the award went to the "Caterham Girls", taking part in their first rally. Sue Bellarby and Kathryn Huddart decided to come on the rally on a whim and bought an open top Caterham 7 just a few days before the start.

The owners of a cleaning agency (Dustintime) had their credit cards and cash stolen in Budapest, forcing them to drive under toll booth barriers for the rest of the route. They broke down seven times between Budapest and Italy and were also stopped seven times for speeding in between (although got away with no fines).

They were continuously lost, got frozen and completely drenched due to their lack of a roof (someone kindly gave them goggles, which they hadn't even brought). Then two hours out of Sicily their Caterham finally blew up, forcing them to hitch hike the whole length of Italy to Monaco!

That's the spirit!

2006 ROUTE

LONDON
BRUXELLES
VIENNA
BUDAPEST
BELGRADE

BANGKOK
PHUKET

11 Rally Stats:
3 Russian Antanov Cargo Planes
1 Iceland Air Boeing 757 Plane
2 Private Jets
120 Cars
250 people
3,000 road miles
18,000 air miles
15 Film Crews
7 Official Photographers
23 Journalists
3,000,000 Gumball Fans

Around the world in 8 days:

1,000 miles Europe:
   Day 1- London
   Day 2- Budapest
   Day 3- Belgrade
1,000 miles Asia:
   Day 4- Phuket
   Day 5- Bangkok
1,000 miles USA:
   Day 6- Salt Lake City
   Day 7- Las Vegas
   Day 8- LA

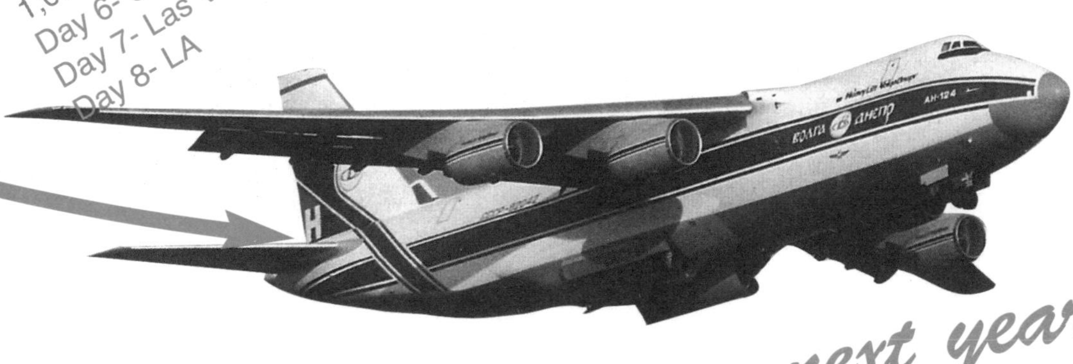

SALT LAKE CITY

LAS VEGAS

LOS ANGELES

See you next year!

ARE YOU THE ULTIMATE GUMBALL FAN?

Is the happy chappy in the green top and beanie you? If you think it is then please send in a photo of yourself to win an Alpinestars bag full of amazing Gumball goodies (all available from our on-line shop at www.gumball3000.com)

Michael Tomlinson

Parting shot....
The Farboud approaches the 90 degree right hander on Pall Mall!